MEDITATIONS FOR HOLY WEEK

Meditations for Holy Week

DYING AND RISING WITH CHRIST

Vassilios Papavassiliou

ANCIENT FAITH PUBLISHING

◊

CHESTERTON, INDIANA

Unless otherwise noted, Scripture quotations are taken
from the New King James Version, © 1979, 1980, 1982 by
Thomas Nelson, Inc. Used by permission.

Published by:
    Ancient Faith Publishing
    (formerly known as Conciliar Press)
    A Division of Ancient Faith Ministries
    P.O. Box 748
    Chesterton, IN 46304

Printed in the United States of America

ISBN 10: 1-936270-88-9
ISBN 13: 978-1-936270-88-0

Second Printing

Contents

Introduction   7

A Guide to Great and Holy Week   13

PART I: THE BRIDEGROOM SERVICE

1 ✢ The Fruits of Repentance   17
GREAT AND HOLY MONDAY

2 ✢ The Noble Joseph   29
GREAT AND HOLY MONDAY

3 ✢ A Litany of Woes   35
GREAT AND HOLY TUESDAY

4 ✢ Increase Your Talent of Grace   41
GREAT AND HOLY TUESDAY

5 ✢ Judas and the Harlot   51
GREAT AND HOLY WEDNESDAY

6 ✢ For Healing of Soul and Body   63
GREAT AND HOLY WEDNESDAY

PART II: THE LORD'S PASSION, DEATH, AND
RESURRECTION

7 ✦ The Eleventh Commandment 69
GREAT AND HOLY THURSDAY

8 ✦ The Humble King 77
GREAT AND HOLY THURSDAY

9 ✦ The Suffering Servant and the
King of Glory 83
GREAT AND HOLY FRIDAY

10 ✦ The Royal Hours and the
Deposition 95
GREAT AND HOLY FRIDAY

11 ✦ Life in the Tomb 103
GREAT AND HOLY SATURDAY

12 ✦ The Descent into Hades and the
Resurrection 109
GREAT AND HOLY SATURDAY

13 ✦ The Great and Holy Sabbath 117
GREAT AND HOLY SATURDAY

14 ✦ Proclaim the Good News 119
GREAT AND HOLY PASCHA

About the Author 133

Introduction

HOLY WEEK, OR GREAT WEEK, is the heart
of the Christian Orthodox Faith and the center
of the yearly cycle of Orthodox feasts. Every year,
our churches are packed at Holy Week, and come
the last three days, they are bursting at the seams
with both those who go to church every Sunday
and those who attend only on special occasions.
Holy Week brings the pious and the not-so-pious
together in a way the most ambitious missionar-
ies can only dream of. But Holy Week does not
stand alone: It follows on from Great Lent, and
the themes of the latter half of Great Lent are
continued in the first half of Holy Week.

Holy Week begins with the first of three Matins services known as the Bridegroom Service. This service belongs to Great and Holy Monday but is usually celebrated on the evening of Palm Sunday. Each liturgical day of the Orthodox Church begins at sunset—the evening prior to the day in question. This practice of reckoning the evening as the beginning of the new day is an ancient Jewish tradition the Church has preserved in its system of worship. In the Creation narrative of Genesis, we read, "So the evening and the morning were the first day" (Gen. 1:5). Therefore, each Sunday begins with Vespers on Saturday evening, followed by Matins in the morning (in monasteries, it is held in the small hours of the morning).

However, in Holy Week, the usual pattern of holding Vespers in the evening and Matins in the morning is typically reversed. Thus in many parishes the evening services of Holy Week are

Matins services, while the morning services are Vespers services.

One could divide Great and Holy Week into two halves. The first half (Great and Holy Monday–Wednesday) is dominated by the Bridegroom Service, which is based on the parable of the ten virgins (Matt. 25:1–13). The image of Christ as the Bridegroom of the Church reminds us of the intimate love and union between God and His people, and the absolute commitment and dedication to Christ that should define our relationship with Him. Many speak of the clergy as being "married to Christ" or "married to the Church," but the image of the Church as the "bride of Christ" reminds us that we are all married to Christ, and therefore complete dedication to Christ and His Church is not the vocation of a select few, but of every member of the Church.

In addition to the central image of the Bridegroom, the first three days of Holy Week are characterized by three key themes: repentance, vigilance, and the Second Coming. The parable of the ten virgins is, after all, a parable about the Last Judgment.

It may seem curious that the Second Coming is a predominant theme, given that Holy Week is all about the First Coming: Christ coming to suffer and die for the world in order to give it new and everlasting life. But the reason for this is fairly straightforward. The Crucifixion, death, and Resurrection of Christ inaugurated the last days. Thus our Lord's final words on the Cross were, "It is finished" (John 19:30). The age of the law has passed, and the age of grace has begun. Through His Resurrection, the life of the age to come has already broken through.

No wonder the early Christians so eagerly anticipated the Lord's Second Coming and spoke of living in the last days. Ever since the Lord ascended to the heavenly Father, there has been nothing left for Christians to do but to carry out the commandments Christ gave us, repent of our sins, proclaim the gospel to all people, and be ready for the Lord to come again. Yet even if the Second Coming is still very far off, the end is at hand for every one of us, since all of us will die. Therefore, the Church never ceases to exhort people of every age to be always ready to meet Christ.

The second half of Holy Week is the commemoration and celebration of our Lord's Passion, Crucifixion, death, burial, and Resurrection. And it is here that we are invited to enter the very essence of Orthodoxy. Holy Week is not simply a religious custom, but the heart of Christianity and the fundamental purpose of the Church in this world: to proclaim the good news that Christ has risen, offering us resurrection to eternal life.

Holy Week is a return to basics, a reintroduction to the very essence of Christian Orthodoxy.

If anyone wishes to learn about the Orthodox Church, there is no better introduction than Holy Week. Here we will find the fundamental doctrines, practices, and ethos of our Church: theology, scripture, worship, prayer, asceticism, repentance, humility, compassion, love. All of this is to be found in abundance in the services of Holy Week, and Orthodox Christians never tire of rediscovering these fundamental beliefs year after year. This little book offers us a glimpse into the profound depth of these seven great and holy days of our Orthodox Church.

A Guide to Great and Holy Week

The Bridegroom Service

Great Monday–Wednesday

(Palm Sunday evening–Great Tuesday evening)

The Liturgy of the Presanctified Gifts

Mornings of Great Monday, Tuesday, and Wednesday

The Curse of the Fig Tree and the Noble Joseph

Great Monday

The Parable of the Ten Virgins

Great Tuesday

The Penitent Harlot

Great Wednesday

Holy Unction

Great Wednesday evening

The Mystical Supper (Vesperal Liturgy of St. Basil)

Great Thursday morning

The Passion and Crucifixion (The Twelve Gospel Readings)

Great Friday (Great Thursday evening)

The Royal Hours and the Deposition (The Taking Down of Christ from the Cross)

Great Friday morning

Christ in the Tomb (The Epitaphios)

Great Saturday (Great Friday evening)

The Descent into Hades and the Resurrection (Vesperal Liturgy of St. Basil)

Great Saturday morning

The Good News (The Paschal Vigil)

Great Saturday night—Pascha morning

Part I

The Bridegroom Service

⊰ 1 ⊱

The Fruits of Repentance

GREAT AND HOLY MONDAY

On this day, like a saving light, the Holy Passion dawns on the world. For Christ in His goodness presses on to His sufferings. Though He holds all creation in the palm of His hand, yet He deigns to be hung on the Cross to save mankind. (First Kathisma of Great Monday Matins)

WHEN THE ICON OF CHRIST the Bridegroom is carried in procession to the center of the Church during the Matins service on the evening of Palm Sunday,[1] we sing:

---

1 Although parishes exist that celebrate Matins in the morning and Presanctified Liturgy in the evening, the opposite practice is so nearly universal that we will refer to it

*Behold, the Bridegroom comes at midnight. And
blessed is the servant whom He shall find watch-
ing. And again, unworthy is the servant whom He
shall find heedless. Beware, therefore, O my soul: do
not be weighed down with sleep, lest you be given
up to death, and lest you be shut out of the Kingdom. But rouse yourself, crying, "Holy, holy, holy, are
You, our God." (Processional hymn, Great Monday
Matins)*

This hymn sums up the central themes of the
first half of Holy Week: vigilance and repentance.
There is a sense of anticipation and urgency
regarding Christ's coming to suffer and die for
the world. The language of the Church here
resembles its warning to be prepared for Christ's
coming again. It is therefore no coincidence that
the Gospel readings we hear at the Liturgy of
the Presanctified Gifts[2] on Great Monday and
Tuesday mornings are about the *Parousia* (the

---

exclusively from here on.

2   The Vesperal Liturgy of weekdays in Lent.

Second Coming). Throughout Holy Week, we are reminded that the Suffering Servant will come again as Judge, and so we are exhorted to repent that we may not be shut out of the "bridal chamber" of Christ (the Kingdom of heaven):

> *Your bridal chamber I see adorned, my Savior, but I have no garment that I may enter. O Giver of Light, make radiant the vesture of my soul and save me. (Exaposteilarion of Great Monday Matins)*

The theme of preparing for Christ by bringing forth the fruit of repentance (Matt. 3:8) is conveyed in very certain terms through the Gospel theme of the cursing of the fig tree, which we hear at the Matins service for Great Monday:

> Now in the morning, as He returned to the city, He was hungry. And seeing a fig tree by the road, He came to it and found nothing on it but leaves, and said to it, "Let no fruit grow on you ever again." Immediately the fig tree withered away. (Matt. 21:18–19)

The exegesis of this seemingly bizarre action is given to us in the Church's hymns:

> The fig tree is compared to the synagogue of the Jews, devoid of spiritual fruit, and Christ withers it with a curse. Let us flee a similar fate. (Synaxarion of Great Monday Matins)

> Mindful of what befell the fig tree, withered for its barrenness, O brethren, let us bear fruits worthy of repentance to Christ, who grants us His great mercy. (Aposticha of Great Monday Matins)

But what are these fruits of repentance? To answer this, let us return to the main hymn of the Bridegroom service (*Behold, the Bridegroom comes at midnight*). This hymn, as we have said, is based on the parable of the ten virgins, which we hear on Great Tuesday morning:

> "Then the kingdom of heaven shall be likened to ten virgins who took their lamps and went out to meet the bridegroom. Now five of them were wise, and five *were* foolish. Those who *were*

foolish took their lamps and took no oil with them, but the wise took oil in their vessels with their lamps. But while the bridegroom was delayed, they all slumbered and slept. And at midnight a cry was *heard:* 'Behold, the bridegroom is coming; go out to meet him!' Then all those virgins arose and trimmed their lamps. And the foolish said to the wise, 'Give us *some* of your oil, for our lamps are going out.' But the wise answered, saying, 'No, lest there should not be enough for us and you; but go rather to those who sell, and buy for yourselves.' And while they went to buy, the bridegroom came, and those who were ready went in with him to the wedding; and the door was shut. Afterward the other virgins came also, saying, 'Lord, Lord, open to us!' But he answered and said, 'Assuredly, I say to you, I do not know you.' Watch therefore, for you know neither the day nor the hour in which the Son of Man is coming." (Matt. 25:1–13)

The parable illustrates the typical custom of marriage among the people of Israel at that time.

After the engagement ceremony, the bridegroom, accompanied by relatives and friends, would make his way to the bride's home, where she would await him in her best attire, surrounded by friends. The wedding ceremony would usually take place at night; therefore, the friends of the bride would meet the bridegroom with lit lamps. Since the exact time of the bridegroom's arrival would not be known, those who were waiting would provide themselves with oil in case it should burn out in the lamps. The bride, with her face covered by a veil, together with the bridegroom and all the participants in the ceremony, would make their way to the bridegroom's house, singing and dancing. The doors would be shut, the marriage contract would be signed, blessings would be pronounced in honor of the couple, the bride would uncover her face, and the marriage feast would begin.

The parable makes it clear that the foolish

virgins had not made the necessary preparation for the bridegroom's coming, and this lack of preparation is conveyed in their lack of oil. The oil represents the virtues, and particularly the virtues of mercy and compassion.

It is telling that some of our Church Fathers and hymn writers, who were great lovers of wordplay, make a comparison between the Greek word for oil, *elaion*, and the Greek word for mercy, *eleos*. And mercy is what the Church recognizes the oil to symbolize in this parable. This is why the foolish virgins cannot take the oil from the wise. Mercy and compassion are virtues we must acquire and labor for. There is no easy or lazy solution. We must bring forth the "fruits of repentance," that is to say, the works that flow from a genuine contrition and conversion, from dedicated vigilance and sincere faith:

Brethren, let us greet the Bridegroom with love, trimming our lamps so that we reflect virtue

and true faith. So shall we be ready, like the pru-
dent maidens of the Lord, to enter with Him into
the wedding feast. For being God, the Bridegroom
bestows on all the gift of an incorruptible crown.
(Kathisma, Matins of Great Tuesday)

I have succumbed to spiritual indolence, O Christ
my Bridegroom, and hold no lamp alight with vir-
tue. I am like the foolish virgins, wandering about
when it was time to act. Master, do not seal against
me the wellsprings of Your pity; but rouse me to
shake off the gloom of sleep and lead me with the
prudent maids into Your bridal chamber. Here the
clear song of those who rejoice can be heard, sing-
ing, "O Lord, glory to You!" (The Praises, Matins of
Great Tuesday)

The fruits of repentance are above all acts of
mercy and compassion, works of humility and
love. If we pay careful attention to the hymns,
themes, and biblical readings of Holy Week, we
will notice that the themes of oil and repentance,
humility and love, emerge time and again in the

Church's services. The foolish virgins' lack of the "oil of mercy" in the parable of the bridegroom vividly reminds us of our Lord's exhortation: "Go and learn what *this* means: 'I desire mercy and not sacrifice'" (Matt. 9:13; see also Hos. 6:6).

To be prepared for the Lord's coming, it is not enough to "*discern* the signs of the times" (Matt. 16:3); there must be a change from within, a conversion to humility, divine love, and mercy. Thus on Great Monday, the Church brings us back to the central theme of the Gospel reading for the fifth Sunday of Lent (Mark 10:32–45), and we are reminded of our Lord's commandment to imitate Him by being humble and loving one another:

> *"All will know you are My disciples if you keep My commandments," said the Lord as He approached His Passion. "Be at peace with yourselves and with everyone; and in your humility you will be exalted. Confessing Me as Lord, sing praise and exaltation forever."*

"Let your ways be contrary to those of the Gentiles and their lords. That is not My inheritance to you; a selfish will is tyranny. So he who would be first among you, let him be the last. Confessing Me as Lord, sing praise and exaltation forever." (Eighth Ode of the Canon of Great Monday Matins)

In Your perfect wisdom, You counseled Your disciples: "Casting off every impure impulse, acquire a prudent mind worthy of the divine Kingdom. Thus shall you be glorified, shining more brightly than the sun."

"Consider Me," You said to Your disciples, Lord, "and do not harbor proud thoughts, but keep company with the meek. The cup that I drink you will drink, and so you will be glorified with Me in the Kingdom of the Father." (Magnificat of Great Monday Matins)

How are we to acquire such an incredible degree of love, compassion, and humility? The answer is given to us in the following hymn:

As the Lord was going to His voluntary Passion, He said to the Apostles on the way, "Behold, we go up to

*Jerusalem, and the Son of Man will be delivered up
as it is written of Him." Come, therefore, let us also
go with Him, purified in mind. Let us be crucified
with Him and die with Him to the pleasures of this
life. Then we shall live with Him and hear Him say,
"I go no more to the earthly Jerusalem to suffer, but
to My Father and your Father; to My God and your
God. And I will raise you up to the Jerusalem on
high, to the kingdom of heaven." (Praises of Great
Monday Matins)*

If we are not willing to endure hardship for God
and neighbor, if we refuse to practice asceticism,
we will always be too weak and selfish to practice
perfect and selfless love. True love and compassion mean self-denial.

Many people are perfectly willing to deny
themselves certain things and make sacrifices for
some greater purpose. An athlete endures physical hardship and observes strict diets in order
to reach and maintain the physical condition
required to succeed in his sport. Others abstain

from certain foods for reasons of health or beauty. Yet tell such people to do the same for Christ, and one is often met with a whole host of objections, with jeering or even anger.

To be Christians means to take up Christ's Cross and follow Him to Golgotha. In other words, we are called to voluntarily sacrifice the pleasures of this life that we may reach and maintain the required spiritual condition to practice self-denying love. We are invited to journey with our Lord to His Passion and death by dying to the self, for it is only by choosing to die with Christ—that is to say, by sacrificing the pleasures of the flesh and the stubbornness of pride and selfishness—that we can rise with Him to the new, transfigured, and everlasting life of the Resurrection.

❧ 2 ❧

The Noble Joseph

GREAT AND HOLY MONDAY

Mindful of your final hour, O soul, and dreading the fate of the fig tree, cultivate with diligence the talent you were given. Endure, be vigilant, and say, "May we not be shut out of the bridal chamber!" (Kontakion, Matins of Great Tuesday)

GREAT AND HOLY MONDAY has two principal themes. The first is the withering of the fig tree, which we touched upon already in the previous chapter. The second is the Patriarch Joseph, whose story can be read in Genesis 37—50. But what is the connection between Joseph and the Passion of Jesus?

Joseph is what is known as a *type* of Jesus. Joseph was one of the twelve sons of Jacob, and the most beloved of the twelve. For this reason, Joseph's brothers despised him. One day, while plotting to get rid of him, one of the brothers, called Judas, suggested they sell Joseph into slavery, which they did for twenty pieces of silver[3] (analogous to the disciple Judas betraying Jesus for thirty pieces of silver). The brothers went on to tell their father that Joseph was killed by a wild beast, which obviously devastated Jacob.

Joseph's life was filled with suffering and persecution. However, due to his gift of interpreting dreams, he came to be in the service of the Egyptian nobleman Potiphar. One day, Potiphar's wife tried to seduce Joseph while he was clad in only a cloth. Joseph resisted, Potiphar's wife grabbed

---

3 This is the reading of the Jewish Old Testament (the Masoretic text). In the Greek Old Testament (the Septuagint), the reading is "twenty pieces of gold"—worth more than the thirty pieces of silver our Lord was sold for.

hold of the cloth, and Joseph ran away naked. She cried rape, and Joseph was arrested.

This story is alluded to in the Gospel when our Lord is arrested in the Garden of Gethsemane:

> Now a certain young man followed Him, having a linen cloth thrown around *his* naked *body*. And the young men laid hold of him, and he left the linen cloth and fled from them naked. (Mark 14:51–52)

The mysterious man in this Gospel narrative points us to the story of Joseph, thus reminding us that all that is to befall Jesus was foretold long ago and is meant to come to pass.

But we must not forget that the story of Joseph has a happy ending, which is again reminiscent of Christ. Joseph rose to become a wise ruler in Egypt. Having made provision for a famine, he supported the needy when the famine struck. Joseph's brothers, who were in need, went to seek Joseph's help (unaware of his true identity and unable to recognize him). After revealing himself, Joseph forgave his fearful brethren, and his father rejoiced as one whose son had risen from the dead. Joseph's forgiving words to his brothers are prophetic of our Lord, who suffered "to give His life a ransom for many" (Mark 10:45), granting us all forgiveness and eternal life through His Cross and Resurrection:

> "Don't be afraid. Am I in the place of God? You intended to harm me, but God intended it for good to accomplish what is now being done, the saving of many lives. So then, don't be afraid. I will provide for you and your children." (Gen. 50:19–21)

In addition to the great significance of Joseph as a type of Christ, there are two important lessons we can draw from his story:

1) *Suffering is not always senseless.* On the contrary, it is often a means of discovering the will of God and coming closer to Him.

Joseph endured unspeakable hardship, injustice, and affliction in a Christlike way, which we should bear in mind when we are troubled by wickedness, unfairness, and pain.

2) *To forgive those who wrong us is to be like Christ.* No one can claim to be a Christian if he does not believe in forgiving those who sin against him and does not at least strive to put what he believes into practice. To be a Christian is to be an imitator of Christ, and to imitate Christ is to forgive our enemies.

It is therefore no wonder that the Patriarch Joseph is one of the principal themes of Great and Holy Monday. For the central themes of Joseph's story are also the central themes of our Lord's Passion: betrayal, suffering, and forgiveness.

↳ 3 ↰

A Litany of Woes

GREAT AND HOLY TUESDAY

Why are you so indifferent, O wretched soul? Why do you appear heedless and uncaring at such a time? Why do you busy yourself with transient things? The end time is upon us, and we shall soon be parted from earthly concerns. While you yet have time, turn sober and confess, "I have sinned against You, my Savior, do not cut me down like the barren fig tree, but as the compassionate Christ have pity on me as I cry out in awe, 'May we not be shut out of the bridal chamber!'" (Oikos, Matins of Great Tuesday)

THE GOSPEL READING of the Matins service for Great Tuesday (Matt. 22:15–46; 23:1–39) includes our Lord's fearful litany of woes upon the scribes and Pharisees. Every year, when I am nearing the end of this long reading, I have to fight to hold back the tears and to keep my voice from breaking. Why do I find our Lord's vehement condemnation of the scribes and Pharisees so moving? Because I know that these harsh words of our Lord are directed at us Christians, and especially at me. If anyone applauds these words of our Lord as words spoken against others, against "them" and not us, we have missed the point of this reading, and we stand self-condemned by our refusal to admit our own hypocrisy:

> "Woe to you, scribes and Pharisees, hypocrites! Because you build the tombs of the prophets and adorn the monuments of the righteous, and say, 'If we had lived in the days of our fathers, we would not have been partakers with them in the blood of the prophets.' Therefore you are witnesses against yourselves that you are sons

of those who murdered the prophets." (Matt.
23:29–31)

We may be tempted to think, "If I had been alive
at the time of Jesus, I would have been one of His
followers, not one of His condemners." But can
we be so sure? We often praise saints who lived
hundreds of years ago for their austerity, their
love of the poor, their condemnation of wealth
and worldly pleasures. But when people of our
own day condemn sin, we accuse them of being
fanatics; when they denounce fundamentalism,
we dismiss them as liberals; when they speak out
against mammon, we dub them socialists; and
when they discourage worldly ways, we mock
them as pastorally insensitive, unsociable, back-
ward, and naïve. It is easy to praise the words of
saints we have never met when we think their
rebukes were aimed at others; but when someone
here and now points out our own sins, it's a whole
other story.

The sad truth that this litany of woes invites us to face up to is this: I am a Pharisee! For we Christians are often guilty of the religious hypocrisy our Lord condemns:

"They bind heavy burdens, hard to bear, and lay *them* on men's shoulders; but they *themselves* will not move them with one of their fingers. But all their works they do to be seen by men. They make their phylacteries broad and enlarge the borders of their garments. They love the best places at feasts, the best seats in the synagogues, greetings in the marketplaces, and to be called by men, 'Rabbi, Rabbi.'" (Matt. 23:4–7)

"But woe to you, scribes and Pharisees, hypocrites! For you shut up the kingdom of heaven against men; for you neither go in *yourselves*, nor do you allow those who are entering to go in. Woe to you, scribes and Pharisees, hypocrites! For you devour widows' houses, and for a pretense make long prayers. Therefore you will receive greater condemnation. Woe to you, scribes and Pharisees, hypocrites! For you travel land and sea to win one proselyte, and when he is won, you make him twice as much a son of hell as yourselves." (Matt. 23:13–15)

"Woe to you, scribes and Pharisees, hypocrites! For you pay tithe of mint and anise and cumin, and have neglected the weightier *matters* of the law: justice and mercy and faith. These you ought to have done, without leaving the others undone. Blind guides, who strain out a gnat and swallow a camel! . . . You are like whitewashed tombs which indeed appear beautiful outwardly, but inside are full of dead *men's* bones and all uncleanness. Even so you also outwardly appear righteous to men, but inside you are full of hypocrisy and lawlessness." (Matt. 23:23–28)

In chapter one, we saw that the principal virtues we require for salvation—those things that make us ready to meet the Lord—are mercy and humility. Now we see that the only sins we need be guilty of to be damned to hell are cold-heartedness and pride: "Serpents, brood of vipers!

How can you escape the condemnation of hell?" (Matt. 23:33).

How indeed? By recognizing our pride and hypocrisy and turning to God in repentance. We all fail to be what God wants us to be, to do those things He asks us to do. But true Christians are not those who never sin and never fail, but rather those who repent of their sins and shortcomings and turn to God in humility. Only when we cast off the blinkers of pride that blind us to the fact that *we* are the cold-hearted and self-righteous hypocrites of the Gospels, whom we so relish mocking and condemning, will we be able to recognize as Lord and God Him who is "gentle and lowly in heart" (Matt. 11:29). Only then can we proclaim, "Blessed *is* He who comes in the name of the LORD!" (Matt. 23:39).

✢ 4 ✢

Increase Your Talent of Grace

GREAT AND HOLY TUESDAY

All who have received a talent from God, increase its grace with the help of Christ who gave it, singing, "All you works of the Lord, praise the Lord!" (Eighth ode of the Canon for Matins of Great Tuesday)

ON GREAT TUESDAY MORNING, the Gospel reading (Matthew 24:36—26:2) provides us with two parables of the Last Judgment. The first is the parable of the ten virgins, which, as we have said before, is the central theme of the first half of Holy Week. The second is the parable of the talents:

> "For *the kingdom of heaven is* like a man traveling to a far country, *who* called his own servants and delivered his goods to them. And to one he gave five talents, to another two, and to another one, to each according to his own ability; and immediately he went on a journey. Then he who had received the five talents went and traded with them, and made another five talents. And likewise he who *had received* two gained two more also. But he who had received one went and dug in the ground, and hid his lord's money.
>
> "After a long time the lord of those servants came and settled accounts with them. So he who had received five talents came and brought five other talents, saying, 'Lord, you delivered to me five talents; look, I have gained five more talents besides them.' His lord said to him, 'Well *done*, good and faithful servant; you were faithful over a few things, I will make you ruler over many things. Enter into the joy of your lord.'
>
> "He also who had received two talents came

and said, 'Lord, you delivered to me two talents; look, I have gained two more talents besides them.' His lord said to him, 'Well *done,* good and faithful servant; you have been faithful over a few things, I will make you ruler over many things. Enter into the joy of your lord.'

"Then he who had received the one talent came and said, 'Lord, I knew you to be a hard man, reaping where you have not sown, and gathering where you have not scattered seed. And I was afraid, and went and hid your talent in the ground. Look, *there* you have *what is* yours.'

"But his lord answered and said to him, 'You wicked and lazy servant, you knew that I reap where I have not sown, and gather where I have not scattered seed. So you ought to have deposited my money with the bankers, and at my coming I would have received back my own with interest. Therefore take the talent from him, and give *it* to him who has ten talents. For to everyone who has, more will be given, and he will have abundance; but from him who does not have, even what he has will be taken away.

And cast the unprofitable servant into the outer darkness. There will be weeping and gnashing of teeth.' (Matt. 25:14–30)

The talents (coins) in this parable represent the gifts and virtues God has given us. As the Gospel and the hymns of Great Tuesday make abundantly clear, we will be judged according to whether we have increased those virtues and responded positively to God's gifts by developing them and sharing them with our fellow human beings:

Come, O faithful, let us work zealously for the Master. For He distributes wealth to His servants. Let each of us, according to his ability, increase his talent of grace. Let one be adorned with wisdom through good works. Let another celebrate a service in splendor. The one communicates the word to the untaught; the other distributes wealth to the poor. Thus we shall increase what has been entrusted to us, and as faithful stewards of grace, we shall be accounted worthy of the Master's joy. Make us worthy of this, O Christ our God, in Your love for mankind. (Aposticha, Matins of Great Tuesday)

Consider, O my soul, the talent the Master entrusts to you. Accept the gift with awe; it is a loan from the giver, so share with the needy, and you will have a friend in the Lord. Thus, when He comes in glory, you may stand at His right hand and hear that blessed voice: "Enter, O servant, into the joy of your Lord!" O my Redeemer, though I have strayed, in Your great mercy count me worthy of that joy. (Aposticha, Matins of Great Tuesday)

As these hymns illustrate, our talent, or talents, could be almost any ability we possess. From an ability to teach to the gift of prayer; from a flair for music to a means of helping the poor, we are all called to recognize what our gifts and abilities are. This means that the first step to increasing our talent of grace is to recognize that we have virtues and abilities in the first place. No one is "talentless."

Yet this simple step is complicated by a

common misconception that it is prideful to acknowledge that one is good at something. This is only prideful if we think ourselves superior because of our abilities. We must recognize our gifts, but we must acknowledge them as divinely given. Unfortunately, many gifted people do become conceited because they forget their virtues and abilities are not of their own making.

If you think about it, such vanity is truly laughable. A woman who is proud of having a high IQ is like a fish being proud of its ability to swim; a man who is proud of his good looks is like a leopard being proud of its spots; a singer who is full of himself because he has a good voice is like a dog being proud of its ability to bark. But it does not therefore follow that an intelligent woman should refuse to recognize her intelligence, or that a handsome man should think of himself as ugly, or that a good singer should live in denial of his ability to sing well.

All that being said, the fundamental question remains: "How, exactly, can I use my abilities for God and His Church?" This is not a question I can hope to answer for each individual, but some examples come to mind. I once knew a Christian doctor who would offer his services for free to one or two people every month. Others have kindly given their time to act as translators for Orthodox immigrants who have not yet learned English. Orthodox Christians who have a gift for music could learn to become cantors or choir directors or singers in our churches. Others are wealthy enough to cover the costs of a church building's repairs or support a parish's soup kitchen for the homeless.

But the parable of the talents should not be understood in such narrow terms—as being concerned only with our gifts and abilities. The talents of this parable represent, above all else, our virtues. There are two main obstacles to increasing in virtue. The first is refusing to recognize that we have any virtues to increase; the second is thinking that having a virtue by nature is somehow sufficient. We must also consider that increasing our talent of grace means not only growing in the virtues we already possess, but also acquiring those virtues we lack.

Consider, for example, two Christians. The first is by nature patient, but he is also by nature a Scrooge; the second is by nature ill-tempered, but he is also by nature generous. If the former thinks to himself, "I'm a patient man—that's good enough," and neither strives to become even more patient than he is by nature nor works on becoming more generous, he has buried his talent in the earth. He can claim no credit for being patient, for his patience is his by nature, by God's grace alone. He did nothing to build upon his natural virtue and surpass what he is by nature, and nothing to acquire the virtue he lacked.

If, on the other hand, the second Christian manages to overcome his ill-tempered nature and become a little more patient, or if he strives to become an even more generous person than he is by nature, then he has increased his talent of grace. He may yet be a less patient man than the first Christian, yet in God's eyes he is the more virtuous, for he labored to become a more patient man than he was by nature. So we must not judge by whether someone is kinder, more patient, more humble, or more restrained than another. For, as the parable makes clear, each person shall be judged not by how many talents he has received, but by whether he has increased them.

This parable is therefore a stern warning neither to be proud of our virtues and abilities nor to bury our talent in the earth out of false modesty. We will all be judged both by our measure of grace and by our works. So consider which virtues you possess, consider what gifts and opportunities you have been given, and build on them. Consider also the virtues you lack, and strive to add them to the virtues you have already. *Thus we shall increase what has been entrusted to us, and as faithful stewards of grace, we shall be accounted worthy of the Master's joy. Make us worthy of this, O Christ our God, in Your love for mankind.*

→ 5 ←

Judas and the Harlot

GREAT AND HOLY WEDNESDAY

The former prodigal suddenly turned chaste, despising the base acts of sin and carnal pleasure, reflecting on the profound shame and the judgment of hell that harlots and wantons suffer. I have become the worst of these and am terrified, yet, fool that I am, I persist in my ugly habit. But the woman taken in sin, troubled and in haste, came crying out to the Redeemer, "O compassionate lover of mankind, free me from the foulness of my deeds." (Oikos, Matins of Great Wednesday)

"WHEREVER THIS GOSPEL is preached in the whole world, what this woman has done will also be told as a memorial to her" (Matt. 26:13). So said our Lord of the penitent harlot who fell before His feet in tears and anointed Him in love. Every Great Wednesday we remember this woman's repentance, and in so doing, we are reminded of our need to repent:

> *Though I have outdone the harlot in sin, yet I have offered You no shower of tears. So I fall before You, fervently kissing Your immaculate feet, praying silently that, as Master, You will remit my debts as I cry, O Savior, "Free me from the foulness of my deeds." (Kontakion, Matins of Great Wednesday)*

While the Gospel passage regarding the penitent harlot on Great Wednesday morning is the reading from Matthew 26:6–16, the Church's hymns on this subject are inspired also by the account in Luke 7:36–50. We find in each narrative two different emphases in the story, which our hymns build upon. The account in Luke's Gospel reveals to us the greatness of Christ's mercy. The harlot's contrition and love alone were sufficient for her salvation. All her sins were washed away in a moment:

Then one of the Pharisees asked Him to eat with him. And He went to the Pharisee's house, and sat down to eat. And behold, a woman in the city who was a sinner, when she knew that *Jesus* sat at the table in the Pharisee's house, brought an alabaster flask of fragrant oil, and stood at His feet behind *Him* weeping; and she began to wash His feet with her tears, and wiped *them* with the hair of her head; and she kissed His feet and anointed them with the fragrant oil. Now when the Pharisee who had invited Him saw *this,* he spoke to himself, saying, "This Man, if He were a prophet, would know who and what manner of woman *this is* who is touching Him, for she is a sinner."

And Jesus answered and said to him, "Simon, I have something to say to you."

So he said, "Teacher, say it."

"There was a certain creditor who had two

debtors. One owed five hundred denarii, and the other fifty. And when they had nothing with which to repay, he freely forgave them both. Tell Me, therefore, which of them will love him more?"

Simon answered and said, "I suppose the *one* whom he forgave more."

And He said to him, "You have rightly judged." Then He turned to the woman and said to Simon, "Do you see this woman? I entered your house; you gave Me no water for My feet, but she has washed My feet with her tears and wiped *them* with the hair of her head. You gave Me no kiss, but this woman has not ceased to kiss My feet since the time I came in. You did not anoint My head with oil, but this woman has anointed My feet with fragrant oil. Therefore I say to you, her sins, which *are* many, are forgiven, for she loved much. But to whom little is forgiven, the *same* loves little."

Then He said to her, "Your sins are forgiven."

And those who sat at the table with Him began to say to themselves, "Who is this who even forgives sins?"

Then He said to the woman, "Your faith has saved you. Go in peace."

This woman's actions were inspired by love. It may be possible that she spent all she had to acquire the precious ointment. But we read in Matthew that the apostles—and in John 12:1–6, Judas—murmured that this was a waste of money that could have been used for the poor.

Many others think the same way: Why waste money on splendid churches and religious devotion when there are so many people in need? But throughout its history, the Church has always stressed the importance of both religious devotion and charity. Both are pleasing to God if they are done in a spirit of love. Our Lord acknowledged the harlot's love for Him in her act of religious devotion. It was also a divinely inspired action, for it was prophetic of His impending burial:

> *A woman pouring myrrh over Christ's body antic-*
> *ipated the embalming by Nicodemus. (Synaxarion,*
> *Matins of Great Wednesday)*

While Luke's narrative emphasizes the love of the harlot and Christ's forgiveness, the reading from Matthew emphasizes the contrast between the penitent harlot and the traitor apostle:

And when Jesus was in Bethany at the house of Simon the leper, a woman came to Him having an alabaster flask of very costly fragrant oil, and she poured *it* on His head as He sat *at the table.* But when His disciples saw *it,* they were indignant, saying, "Why this waste? For this fragrant oil might have been sold for much and given to *the* poor."

But when Jesus was aware of *it,* He said to them, "Why do you trouble the woman? For she has done a good work for Me. For you have the poor with you always, but Me you do not have always. For in pouring this fragrant oil on My body, she did *it* for My burial. Assuredly, I say to you, wherever this gospel is preached in the whole world, what this woman has done will also be told as a memorial to her."

Then one of the twelve, called Judas Iscariot, went to the chief priests and said, "What are you willing to give me if I deliver Him to you?" And they counted out to him thirty pieces of silver. So from that time he sought opportunity to betray Him. (Matt. 26:6–16)

Our hymns, while praising the repentance of the harlot, at the same time express our bewilderment at the betrayal of Judas, who lived with Christ, ate with Him, witnessed His miracles, heard His words, and even worked miracles in Christ's name (Matt. 10:1–4):

What was it, O Judas, that turned you into the Savior's betrayer? Did He separate you from the fellowship of the Apostles? Did He withhold from you His healing grace? Did He banish you from the table when you all supped together? When He washed the feet of the others, did He overlook yours?

Oh, how many blessings you have forgotten! And so your ingratitude will be inscribed in history, while His unfathomable forbearance and great mercy will forever be proclaimed. (Kathisma of the sixth antiphon of Great Friday)

As the sinful woman was offering myrrh, the disciple was scheming with lawless men. She rejoiced in pouring out her precious gift; he hastened to sell the precious One. She acknowledged the Master; he departed from Him. She was set free, but Judas was enslaved to the enemy. How terrible his indolence! How great her repentance! O Savior, who suffered for our sakes, grant us her repentance and save us. (Hymn of the Praises, Matins of Great Wednesday)

The hymns of our Church always lay before us the example of penitents who found salvation, revealing the contrast between them and the elect who fell from grace, the proud "insiders" who secretly hated God. The above hymn reminds us of the Communion hymn we often hear at Divine

Liturgy (which was initially the Communion hymn only of Great Thursday morning):

> *Of Your mystical supper, O Son of God, receive me today as a communicant, for I will not tell of the Mystery to Your enemies; I will not give You a kiss, like Judas, but like the Thief I confess You: "Remember me, Lord, in Your Kingdom."*

We are thus reminded that being "insiders" and members of Christ's Church in no way guarantees our salvation. As our Lord said, after praising the faith of the pagan centurion, "I say to you that many will come from east and west, and sit down with Abraham, Isaac, and Jacob in the kingdom of heaven. But the sons of the kingdom will be cast out into outer darkness" (Matt. 8:11–12).

Thus the Church emphatically warns us that we too can be traitors of Christ, while those we condemn and ostracize may have greater faith, love, and repentance than we do.

✢ THE HYMN OF KASSIANI ✢

The theme of the penitent harlot reaches its climax on Great Tuesday evening with the famous and beloved hymn of St. Kassiani, a Byzantine nun, poet, and hymnographer. Few hymns move Orthodox Christians as much as this adored composition. In the Byzantine tradition, the music for the hymn is slow and sorrowful; it is considered one of the most demanding pieces of Byzantine chant. Cantors take great pride in singing it well, while some Orthodox Christians make a point of going to the service of Great Tuesday evening specifically to listen to this hymn:

> Lord, the woman caught up in a multitude of sins, sensing Your divinity, assumes the perfumer's role; lamenting, she provides myrrh in anticipation of Your burial. "Alas!" she cries, "for me night is a frenzy of excess, dark and moonless, a love affair with sin. You draw from the clouds the waters of the sea; will You accept the fountainhead of my tears?

In Your inexpressible condescension You made the heavens incline; incline now to the groaning of my heart. I will cover Your immaculate feet with kisses, then dry them with my tresses. Eve heard Your footsteps in Paradise and hid herself in fear. Who can fathom the magnitude of my transgressions or the depths of Your judgments, O Savior of my soul? Yet in Your boundless mercy do not reject me, Your servant. (The Hymn of St. Kassiani, Doxastikon of Matins of Great Wednesday)

In addition to its poetic and penitential character, this moving hymn provides us with a couple of profound theological references to the Old Testament that place Christ at the beginning of the Creation narrative. This reminds us that Jesus is no mere mortal, but the pre-eternal Son of God "through whom all things were made" (the Nicene Creed):

You draw from the clouds the waters of the sea; will You accept the fountainhead of my tears? In Your inexpressible condescension You made the heavens

incline; incline now to the groaning of my heart. . . .
Eve heard Your footsteps in Paradise and hid herself
in fear.

Such language is typical of Orthodox hymnology, particularly in Holy Week. We are invited to reflect upon the paradox of Christ's divinity and humanity; His eternity and mortality; His majesty and humility; His almighty power and tender mercy. We fear Him above all others, and we love Him above all others; He is our judgment and our salvation; against Him alone we have sinned, but Him alone we adore. And so, with St. Kassiani and the penitent harlot, we cry: *Who can fathom the magnitude of my transgressions or the depths of Your judgments, O Savior of my soul? Yet in Your boundless mercy do not reject me, Your servant.*

⇥ 6 ⇤

For Healing of Soul and Body

GREAT AND HOLY WEDNESDAY

Anointed with spiritual myrrh, O Christ our God, free us from the passions that overwhelm us and be merciful to us, for You alone are holy and love mankind. (Synaxarion, Matins of Great Wednesday)

HAVING COMMEMORATED Christ's anointing, it is fitting that we too should be anointed, and so, on Great Wednesday evening, we have the Sacrament of Holy Unction—in Greek, *Euchelaion* (Prayer of Oil). This sacrament of the Church is for healing of both soul and body—for forgiveness of sins as well as physical healing. The oldest reference to this sacrament is found in the Epistle of St. James (c. AD 47):

> Is anyone among you sick? Let him call for the elders of the church, and let them pray over him, anointing him with oil in the name of the Lord. And the prayer of faith will save the sick, and the Lord will raise him up. And if he has committed sins, he will be forgiven. (5:14–15)

The Euchelaion Service includes seven epistle readings and seven Gospel readings, many of which refer to passages concerning oil, mercy, and healing. As we gather together for this sacrament to pray, to hear the Scriptures, and to be anointed with the holy oil, we are reminded of the intimate union of soul and body, of how the miracles of healing wrought by our Lord were always accompanied by the announcement of forgiveness:

> *The whole earth is full of Your mercy, O Master.*
> *Therefore, as we are mystically anointed with holy*

oil this day, in faith we implore You that we may be shown Your mercy, which is beyond understanding. (Canon of the Service of Holy Unction, first ode, Great Wednesday evening)

The Euchelaion Service expresses the soul's deep yearning for spiritual healing, which is the purpose of repentance. The repentance of Great Lent consumes both body and soul and finds its expression in physical and spiritual fasting. It is therefore fitting that forgiveness should also be conveyed in a physical and tangible form—through the anointing of our bodies. Just as our Lord's anointing was a preparation for His Passion and burial, so too is our anointing a preparation for the spiritual journey to Calvary and the burial of our passions.

But let us not forget that our Lord's forgiveness was often followed by a commandment: "Go and sin no more." Having received forgiveness, let us be thankful for God's boundless mercy, and let us strive not to sin again. For true repentance is a change of heart and the beginning of a new life. It finds joy and fulfillment in divine forgiveness, which should soften our hearts and fill us with gratitude. Thus the oil with which we are anointed is called "the oil of gladness":

> *By anointing the heads of all with the anointment of oil, give the joy of gladness to those who seek the mercy of Your redemption in Your abundant mercy, O Lord. (Canon of the Service of Holy Unction, seventh ode, Great Wednesday evening)*

Part II

The Lord's Passion, Death, and Resurrection

⇥ 7 ⇤

The Eleventh Commandment

GREAT AND HOLY THURSDAY

Let us all approach the mystical table in fear, and with pure souls let us receive the Bread. Let us stay at the Master's side that we may see how He washes the feet of the disciples and wipes them with a towel; and let us do as we have seen, subjecting ourselves to each other and washing one another's feet. For such is the commandment that Christ gave to His disciples. (Ikos of Great Thursday Matins)

$\mathcal{A}$FTER GREAT WEDNESDAY, we move on from the theme of the Bridegroom, and on

Great Thursday a Vesperal Liturgy of St. Basil the Great[4] is held as we celebrate the Mystical Supper, the very first Eucharist. The narrative of the appointed Gospel reading[5] includes our Lord washing the feet of His disciples, the betrayal of Judas, and the arrest of Jesus. But the central theme of the day is our Lord's Last Supper.

The Last Supper replaced and fulfilled the Jewish Passover, which commemorated the liberation of the Hebrew people from slavery in Egypt to freedom in the Promised Land and their salvation from the plague of death in Egypt:

> Now the LORD spoke to Moses and Aaron in the land of Egypt, saying, ". . . every man shall

---

4 The first half of the Liturgy through the Old Testament readings is a Vespers service. What follows is the Divine Liturgy from the Trisagion hymn ("Holy God, Holy Mighty One, Holy Immortal, have mercy on us").

5 Although the liturgical text states that the reading is from the Gospel according to Matthew, it is in fact an amalgamation of the Gospels of Matthew, Luke, and John: Matt. 26:2–20; John 13:3–17; Matt. 26:21–34; Luke 22:43–45; Matt. 26:40—27:2.

take for himself a lamb. . . . Your lamb shall be without blemish, a male of the first year. . . . I will pass through the land of Egypt . . . and will strike all the firstborn in the land of Egypt, both man and beast; and against all the gods of Egypt I will execute judgment: I *am* the LORD. Now the blood shall be a sign for you on the houses where you *are*. And when I see the blood, I will pass over you; and the plague shall not be on you to destroy *you* when I strike the land of Egypt. So this day shall be to you a memorial; and you shall keep it as a feast to the LORD throughout your generations. You shall keep it as a feast by an everlasting ordinance." (Ex. 12:1, 3, 5, 12–14)

Christ is the true Lamb of God, by whose Blood we are delivered from death, and so "the Lord's Passover" (Ex. 12:11) finds its fulfillment in the death of Jesus, which is anticipated and announced in advance in the Mystical Supper:

The Lord, the King of all and our Creator God, has been clothed in our human nature without undergoing change; He Himself is our Passover and has offered Himself to those whom He wished to save by His death: "Take and eat, this is My Body; you shall find food for your faith."

O God most good, You Yourself filled the cup of joy that frees the human race; You offer Yourself in sacrifice, and You make Your disciples drink from it, saying, "Take and drink, this is My Blood; you shall find food for your faith." (Third ode of the Canon of Great Thursday Matins)

In the bread and wine, our Lord illustrated His love for us and vividly portrayed what He was about to endure for our sakes: He broke the bread and said, "This is My body which is given for you; do this in remembrance of Me" (Luke 22:19); and He gave the cup of wine and said, "This is My blood of the new covenant, which is shed for many for the remission of sins" (Matt. 26:28). Our Lord's injunction, "Do this in remembrance of Me," refers not only to the celebration of the

Eucharist, but also to the imitation of His divine love and sacrifice:

> "A new commandment I give to you, that you love one another; as I have loved you, that you also love one another. By this all will know that you are My disciples, if you have love for one another." (John 13:34–35)

> "Greater love has no one than this, than to lay down one's life for his friends." (John 15:13)

The Eucharist is the ultimate expression of divine love, a love we are called to imitate if we are truly to be His disciples. As St. Paul writes:

> For as often as you eat this bread and drink this cup, you proclaim the Lord's death till He comes. Therefore whoever eats this bread or drinks *this* cup of the Lord in an unworthy manner will be guilty of the body and blood of the Lord. But let a man examine himself, and so let him eat of the bread and drink of the cup. (1 Cor. 11:26–28)

We celebrate the Liturgy, yet we do not wish to follow the example of Christ's love given to us in the Eucharist. When we receive Holy Communion, we receive *Love*—pure, selfless, undying, divine *Love*. And yet we so often receive it with indifference, and maybe even with pride and hatred in our hearts. "Do this in remembrance of Me" means not only to "eat this bread and drink this cup" to "proclaim the Lord's death till He comes," not only to "keep it as a feast by an everlasting ordinance"; it means also, "Love one another as I have loved you."

If we do not have Christ's love in our hearts; if we put ourselves first and not last; if we wish to be served rather than to serve, we betray the very meaning of the Lord's Supper. Love and Liturgy must not and cannot be separated. Love without the Liturgy has no context, no point of reference, no real meaning; but the Liturgy without love is nothing but empty ritual and hypocrisy. The eleventh commandment is a double injunction: "Love one another as I have loved you"; "Do this in remembrance of Me." Therein lies the very essence of the Eucharist; therein lies the full meaning of Christian love.

❧ 8 ❧

The Humble King

GREAT AND HOLY THURSDAY

When the glorious disciples were enlightened at the washing of the feet before the supper, then the impious Judas was darkened, ailing with avarice, and to the lawless judges he betrays You, the Righteous Judge. Behold, O lover of money, this man who because of money hanged himself! Flee from the greedy soul that dared such things against the Master! O Lord, who are good towards men, glory to You! (Troparion of Great Thursday Matins)

DURING THE GOSPEL READING of Great Thursday morning, we hear how Christ, before the Mystical Supper, washed the feet of His Disciples:

> Now before the Feast of the Passover, when Jesus knew that His hour had come that He should depart from this world to the Father, having loved His own who were in the world, He loved them to the end. And supper being ended, the devil having already put it into the heart of Judas Iscariot, Simon's *son*, to betray Him, Jesus, knowing that the Father had given all things into His hands, and that He had come from God and was going to God, rose from supper and laid aside His garments, took a towel and girded Himself. After that, He poured water into a basin and began to wash the disciples' feet, and to wipe *them* with the towel with which He was girded.
>
> Then He came to Simon Peter. And *Peter* said to Him, "Lord, are You washing my feet?" Jesus answered and said to him, "What I am doing you do not understand now, but you will know after this." Peter said to Him, "You shall never wash my feet!" Jesus answered

him, "If I do not wash you, you have no part with Me." Simon Peter said to Him, "Lord, not my feet only, but also *my* hands and *my* head!" (John 13:1–9)

Washing someone's feet is hardly a task fit for a king; rather, it belongs to the lowliest slave. And our Lord teaches us that if He, the King and Master of all, is willing to humble Himself and make Himself the servant of all, then all Christians, however exalted their role or office within the Church, should do the same:

So when He had washed their feet, taken His garments, and sat down again, He said to them, "Do you know what I have done to you? You call Me Teacher and Lord, and you say well, for *so* I am. If I then, *your* Lord and Teacher, have washed your feet, you also ought to wash one another's feet. For I have given you an example, that you should do as I have done to you. Most assuredly, I say to you, a servant is not greater than his master; nor is he who is sent greater than he who sent him. If you know these things, blessed are you if you do them." (John 13:12–17)

It is for this reason that when a bishop is present at the Liturgy on Great Thursday, during the Gospel reading he performs a dramatic reenactment of what our Lord did by washing the feet of his clergy and other members of the congregation. For Christ said that "whoever desires to become great among you, let him be your servant. And whoever desires to be first among you, let him be your slave" (Matt. 20:26–27). The bishop holds the highest office in the Church. He is Christ's representative and stands in the place of our Lord, who, in His own words, "did not come to be served, but to serve, and to give His life a ransom for many" (Matt. 20:28). Therefore, bishops ought to do the same.

When we consider what Christ did, how much He condescended and humbled Himself, how can any one claim that anything is beneath him? Who can complain that he is not treated with respect or that his dignity has been compromised? When we remember our Lord washing the feet of mere mortal men, we will know it is quite wrong to think anything or anyone is beneath us.

> *May Christ our true God, who in His surpassing goodness showed us in the washing of the disciples' feet the most excellent way of humility . . . have mercy on us and save us, for He is good and loves mankind. (Dismissal of the Liturgy of Great Thursday)*

⇥ 9 ⇤

The Suffering Servant and the King of Glory

GREAT AND HOLY FRIDAY

The One Isaiah proclaimed to be the Lamb[6] comes willingly to the slaughter. He bares His back to the lash, His cheeks to the strikes. Spat upon, He does not turn away from the humiliation.[7] Willingly the sinless One endures all, that to all He may grant us resurrection from the dead. (Hymn of the stichera, Vespers of Great Thursday)

DURING THE LONG and arduous Matins service for Great Friday, we hear twelve lengthy

---

6   Isaiah 53:7
7   Isaiah 50:6

Gospel readings which are the accounts of our Lord's arrest, trial, humiliation, suffering, and execution. Some ask, "Why so many long readings about the same story? Why so much repetition?"

My answer is that, in my own experience—at least as a priest—we need this service to be exhausting. It is precisely because it is long and tiring that just about every participant—and particularly the clergy—tends to become emotional at some point in this service: we need to be worn down until we begin to feel what we are hearing. I have come to need this tiredness, this very small degree of struggle, to really experience Great Friday. One of the hymns of the day sums it up perfectly:

Lord, as You approached Your voluntary Passion, You declared to Your disciples, "If you could not keep vigil with Me for but one hour, how could you have vowed to die for Me? Look at Judas, how he does not sleep, but hastens to deliver Me to the lawless. Arise and pray, that none of you deny Me when you see Me on the cross." (Sixth Antiphon of Great Friday Matins)

How can we claim that we are willing to live and die for Christ when we cannot even cope with a long church service? As we saw at the beginning of Holy Week, we are invited to *be crucified* with Christ and for Him *to die to the pleasures of this life:*

Let us present our senses purified to Christ, and as His friends, let us offer our lives to Him. Let us not be like Judas, overwhelmed by worldly concerns, but in the quiet of our chambers let us cry, "Our Father in heaven, deliver us from the evil one." (First Antiphon of Great Friday Matins)

Such mortification of our passions cannot be experienced in comfort and convenience, but only in strain and effort.

❖ GOD ON THE CROSS ❖

While the main focus of the first half of the service on Great Thursday evening is our vigilance and preparation for the Crucifixion of our Lord, the second half is more theological. The most significant aspect of Great Friday is not how much our Lord suffered, but who this suffering servant is: the Second Person of the Holy Trinity. He was there at the beginning of Creation; He is the Almighty God of the Old Testament, as the following hymn makes abundantly clear:

> *Today the Jews nail to the Cross the Lord who parted the sea with a staff and led them through the wilderness.[8] Today they pierce with a lance the side of Him who for their sake smote Egypt with plagues.[9] And they give gall to drink to Him who rained down manna on them for food.[10] (Sixth Antiphon of Great Friday Matins)*

---

8 Exodus 13—14
9 Exodus 7—12
10 Exodus 16

A similar hymn, and undoubtedly the best-known hymn of Great Friday, is the one that is chanted during and following the somber procession of the Crucifix after the fifth Gospel reading:

> Today, He who hung the earth upon the waters is
>   hung upon a tree.
> The King of angels is decked with a crown of thorns.
> He who wraps the heavens in clouds is wrapped in
>   the purple of mockery.
> He who freed Adam in the Jordan is struck on
>   the face.
> The Bridegroom of the Church is affixed to the cross
>   with nails.
> The Son of the Virgin is pierced by a spear.
> We worship Your Passion, O Christ.
> Show us also Your glorious Resurrection.
> (Fifteenth Antiphon of Great Friday Matins)

It is worth noting here the reference to the Resurrection. The Orthodox Church on Great Friday does not think of Christ's human pain and suffering in isolation. We marvel at the paradox of God suffering on the Cross—the strange contrast between His humiliation and His eternal glory. The Crucifixion is not about the suffering of a good man; it is about the suffering of God Himself. Behind the image of this broken and humiliated figure, the Church still discerns the Second Person of the Holy Trinity.

The Crucifixion, burial, and Resurrection are all seen as one action, and therefore, even in the Crucifixion itself, we already sense victory. The Resurrection is inevitable. This person on the Cross is mortal only in His humanity; in His divinity He is eternal. He is the giver of life, the source of life. Death is contrary to His divine nature. The Crucifixion can end in only one way: Resurrection. It is not wishful thinking. It does not come to us as a surprise. The Church on Great Friday awaits the Resurrection with eager expectation.

The paradox of the King of Glory suffering

on the Cross becomes yet more explicit after the ninth Gospel reading, when we hear this slow, somber hymn:

> They have stripped Me of My garments
> And have clothed Me in a scarlet robe.
> They have set upon My head a crown of thorns
> And have given Me a reed in My right hand. . . .[11]
> (Doxastikon of the Praises, Great Friday
> Matins)

Here we have an uncompromising expression of Christ's humiliation, but come the last line, the focus shifts entirely:

> That I might smash them in pieces, like a potter's
> vessel.

Of course, our Lord did not say this, but rather, "Father, forgive them, for they do not know what they do" (Luke 23:34). The hymn is poetic and attempts to illustrate how those who mocked

---

11 Matthew 27:27–29

Christ unknowingly expressed a fundamental truth: Jesus is indeed the King of Glory. In the scarlet robe with which the soldiers sought to ridicule Him, the Church sees His majesty; in the crown of thorns, His regal coronet of eternal rule; in the reed, His kingly scepter.

The last line regarding the potter's vessel is a reference to the following Old Testament passage concerning the Son of God:

> I will declare the decree:
> The LORD has said to Me,
> "You *are* My Son,
> Today I have begotten You.
> Ask of Me, and I will give *You*
> The nations *for* Your inheritance,
> And the ends of the earth *for* Your
>   possession.
> You shall break them with a rod of iron;
> You shall dash them to pieces like a potter's vessel." (Ps. 2:7–9)[12]

---

12 See also Rev. 2:27.

Even now, in this utterly humiliated man, the Church still perceives the King of Glory coming to judge the world.

✢ THE PSALM OF THE CROSS ✤

One particular passage of the Gospel, in my experience, always stirs emotion on Great Friday. It is our Lord's cry on the Cross: "My God, My God, why have You forsaken Me?" (Matt. 27:46).

This cry has been a subject of debate among Christians for centuries. Some ask, "Did He really feel the Father had abandoned Him? Did He lose faith? Is this not a denial of His own divinity? Or was it simply a cry of pain?"

It was indeed a cry of pain. Christ was fully human, as well as fully God. The only gospels that present a Christ who felt no pain on the Cross are the heretical Gnostic gospels of the second to fourth centuries, the authors of which believed

Jesus was not really flesh and blood. Yet as important as Jesus' human pain is, there is yet more to this passage. Our Lord was quoting the opening line of Psalm 22 (Psalm 21 LXX), and many of the earliest Christians (the Jewish people) would have recognized it immediately. Why is our Lord citing this psalm? Because it is a prophecy of His crucifixion:

> But I *am* a worm, and no man;
> A reproach of men, and despised by the people.
> All those who see Me ridicule Me;
> They shoot out the lip, they shake the head,
>   *saying,*
> "He trusted in the LORD, let Him rescue Him;
> Let Him deliver Him, since He delights in Him!"
>   (vv. 6–8)[13]

> They gape at Me with their mouths,
> Like a raging and roaring lion.
> I am poured out like water,[14]

---

13 Matthew 27:29–43
14 John 19:34

And all My bones are out of joint;
My heart is like wax;
It has melted within Me.
My strength is dried up like a potsherd,
And My tongue clings to My jaws;[15]
You have brought Me to the dust of death.
For dogs have surrounded Me;
The congregation of the wicked has enclosed
   Me.
They pierced My hands and My feet;
I can count all My bones.
They look and stare at Me.
They divide My garments among them,
And for My clothing they cast lots.[16]
   (vv. 13–18)

Our Lord's cry, "My God, My God, why have You forsaken Me?" is a pointer to Psalm 21/22, which is a clear reminder that our Lord was crucified by His own will. For centuries, too many Christians have looked upon the Crucifixion as a tragedy,

---

15 John 10:28–30
16 John 19:23–24

and they have despised and hated those who put Jesus to death. In so doing, they have completely ignored the very clear biblical teaching that the Crucifixion was not a murder for which we must seek justice, but a voluntary sacrifice in order that we may all have forgiveness. As our Lord said:

> "My Father loves Me, because I lay down My life that I may take it again. No one takes it from Me, but I lay it down of Myself. I have power to lay it down, and I have power to take it again." (John 10:17–18)

⇥ 10 ⇤

The Royal Hours and the Deposition

GREAT AND HOLY FRIDAY

Today a tomb holds Him who holds all creation in His hand. A stone covers Him who covered the heavens with glory. Life sleeps and Hell trembles, and Adam is being released from his bonds. Glory to Your dispensation, through which You have accomplished all things and granted us an eternal Sabbath rest, Your resurrection from the dead! (Hymn of the Praises, Matins of Great Saturday)

⇥ THE ROYAL HOURS ⇤

ON GREAT FRIDAY MORNING, we hear the Royal Hours, a service filled with biblical readings concerning the prophecies of our Lord's Passion and their fulfillment in the New Testament. The main reflection of the day is the paradox of deicide. How can God, who by His very nature is eternal and unable to suffer, suffer and die? While we know that all that Christ endured was by His own will, that it was foretold in the Law, the Psalms, and the Prophets, and that so too was the Resurrection; at the same time the Church invites us to place ourselves at the foot of the Cross and to consider the horror of what happened.

The Cross, burial, and Resurrection of our Lord are called *His three-day work (Dismissal of Pascha)*: they should not be thought of in isolation. Our mourning is tempered with theological certainty; our sorrow with joy; our horror with hope. Nor is our experience of Great Friday to take place in a spiritual vacuum; it should move us to repentance and to the imitation of Christ's divine love. This is powerfully conveyed in St. Theodore the Studite's catechesis for Great Friday, which is read in monasteries during the Royal Hours:

> Let us . . . be amazed in a manner worthy of God, by being changed with a fair change; let us draw down tears, sacrifice the passions, changing insults for insults and exchanging wounds for wounds, the one through obedience, the other through unflinching confession. Do we not see the burning incitements of divine love? Who ever dwelt in prison for a friend? Who accepted slaughter for their beloved? But our good God not only did the one and both of them, but accepted ten thousand sufferings for the sake of us, the condemned.[17]

---

17 *Catechesis 73, On the Saving Passion of our Lord and Master Jesus Christ.* Translation by Fr. Ephrem Lash: http://www.anastasis.org.uk/HWFri-Hrs.htm

✦ THE SERVICE OF THE DEPOSITION ✦

The Hours are immediately followed by Vespers, during which we have the Deposition (the taking down of Christ from the cross and His burial). The previous evening, the crucifix was carried in procession and placed in the center of the church. Now the figure of the Crucified is removed from the cross during the Gospel reading,[18] at the end of which we hear this passage:

Now when evening had come, there came a rich man from Arimathea, named Joseph, who himself had also become a disciple of Jesus. This man went to Pilate and asked for the body of Jesus. Then Pilate commanded the body to be given to him. When Joseph had taken the body, he wrapped it in a clean linen cloth, and laid it in his new tomb which he had hewn out of the

18 The reading from "the holy Gospel according to Matthew" is an amalgamation of the following passages: Matt. 27:1–38; Luke 23:39–43; Matt. 27:39–54; John 19:31–37; Matt. 27:55–61.

rock; and he rolled a large stone against the door of the tomb, and departed. (Matt. 27:57–60)

At this point, the priest takes the image of the Crucified, wraps it in a cloth, and takes it into the sanctuary behind the icon screen, where it will remain until the Feast of the Ascension. Then the *epitaphios*—an icon depicting Christ in the tomb embroidered upon a large cloth—is carried to a special altar decorated with flowers, which represents the new tomb in which our Lord was laid, and we sing:

> When from the Tree the Arimathean took You down as a dead body, O Christ, who are the life of all, he buried You with myrrh and a shroud; and with love he embraced Your immaculate body with heart and lips; yet, shrouded with fear, he cried out to You, rejoicing, "Glory to Your condescension, O Lover of mankind!"
>
> When in the new tomb You, the Redeemer of all, had been laid for the sake of all, Hell became a laughingstock; seeing You, he quaked with fear;

the bars were smashed, the gates were shattered, the graves were opened, the dead arose; then Adam with thanksgiving cried out to You, rejoicing, "Glory to Your condescension, O Lover of mankind!"

When in the tomb in the flesh You were enclosed by Your own will, O Christ, who by the nature of Your Godhead are indescribable and unbounded, You unlocked the storehouses of Hell and emptied all his palaces; then You also bestowed upon this Sabbath Your divine blessing and glory and Your own splendor. (Aposticha of Vespers for Great Friday)

Our preparation for the new and Great and Holy Sabbath has begun. On the first Sabbath day (Gen. 2:2), our Lord, being one of the Trinity, rested from the work of creation. Now, on this new Sabbath, He rests from the work of His earthly ministry. At the beginning of creation, God hallowed the Sabbath day; now He hallows death by His own death and burial. Adam died because of His disobedience (Gen. 2:17); but Christ died in obedience to the Father (Phil. 2:8).

What was the curse of death has now become the gift of new life. For as He is God, death has no power over Him.

Thus the service of the Deposition leads us from the sorrow of Great Friday to the joyful sorrow of Great Saturday, when we ponder the mystery of "Life in the tomb" and celebrate our Lord's descent into the kingdom of death on the Great and Holy Sabbath.

⤖ 11 ⬸

Life in the Tomb

GREAT AND HOLY SATURDAY

Come, let us see our life lying in a tomb, that He may give life to all those who lie in the tombs. Come today, and as we contemplate the sleeping one from Judah, let us prophetically cry out to Him, "Taking Your rest, You lie down like a lion. Who will rouse You, O King? But arise by Your own will, who gave Yourself willingly for us. O Lord, glory to You!" (Hymn of the Praises, Matins of Great Saturday)

THE MATINS SERVICE of Great Saturday (the Service of the Epitaphios on Great Friday evening) can be considered a funeral service for Christ, yet it is the most colorful service of Holy

Week. For Great Friday evening is when the sorrow of the Cross is gradually transformed into the joy of the Resurrection. We sing the Lamentations (undoubtedly among the most beloved hymns of the Orthodox Church), yet somehow everything is bright and joyful. For human life is being born anew in the tomb:

> *O Life, how is it that You die? How is it that You dwell in a tomb? Yet You lay low the reign of death and raise up the dead in Hades. (Hymn of the first stanza of the Lamentations)*

> *Fearsome Hades was utterly shaken when it beheld You, immortal sun of glory, and hastily surrendered its captives. (Hymn of the second stanza of the Lamentations)*

> *The deceiver is deceived, and the one he had deceived is freed, O God, by Your wisdom. (Hymn of the third stanza of the Lamentations)*

> *O happy tomb! For having received in itself the Creator as one asleep, it has been revealed as a treasure*

house of life for the salvation of us who sing, "Blessed are You, O God, our Redeemer!"

The life of all things accepts being laid in the tomb, according to the law of those who die, and He shows it to be a source of rising for the salvation of us who sing, "Blessed are You, O God, our Redeemer!" (Seventh ode of the Canon of Matins for Great Saturday)

Our joyful sorrow is shared with the outside world when we go out into the streets in a procession with the altar of the *epitaphios*, often bearing an inscription that concisely sums up the strange mystery we are at the same time both mourning and celebrating: *Life in the Tomb (Hymn of the first stanza of the Lamentations)*. We mourn because Jesus has died; we celebrate because in so doing He has transformed death into new life for all humanity.

This is why St. Paul writes, "I do not want you to be ignorant, brethren, concerning those who have fallen asleep, lest you sorrow as others who have no hope. For if we believe that Jesus died and rose again, even so God will bring with Him those who sleep in Jesus" (1 Thess. 4:13–14).

The Living God has turned death into life, and so in dying we follow Him to the Resurrection. Death is but a sleep from which we shall all one day awake. So let bereavement be tempered with hope, and let the fear of death be tempered with the joy of knowing that God awaits all those who love Him. For by His death, Resurrection, and Ascension into heaven, our Lord paved a road for humanity to God the Father, a road which, through death, all of us can follow. As our Lord said to the apostles before His Passion:

"Let not your heart be troubled; you believe in God, believe also in Me. In My Father's house are many mansions; if *it* were not *so*, I would have told you. I go to prepare a place for you. And if I go and prepare a place for you, I will come again and receive you to Myself; that where I am, *there* you may be also. And where I go you know, and the way you know." (John 14:1–4)

~ 12 ~

The Descent into Hades and the Resurrection

GREAT AND HOLY SATURDAY

Hell has been wounded, having received in its heart the One whose side was pierced by a lance, and consumed by divine fire, he groans aloud at the salvation of us who sing, "Blessed are You, O God, our Redeemer!" (Seventh ode of the Canon of Matins for Great Saturday)

IF GREAT FRIDAY EVENING is when the sorrow of Great Friday becomes joyful sorrow, then the Vesperal Liturgy of St. Basil the Great on Great Saturday is when joy overwhelms sorrow. For we celebrate the harrowing of hell, the vanquishing of death, and our Lord's Resurrection from the tomb. This is aptly expressed in the poetic hymns of Vespers for Great Saturday:

Today Hell cries out groaning, "I should not have accepted the Man born of Mary. He came and destroyed my power. He shattered the gates of brass. As God, He raised the souls that I held captive." Glory to Your Cross and Resurrection, O Lord.

Today, Hell cries out groaning, "My dominion has been shattered. I received a mortal man as one of the dead, but against Him I could not prevail. From eternity I had ruled the dead, but behold, He raises all. Because of Him I perish." Glory to Your Cross and Resurrection, O Lord.

Today, Hell cries out groaning, "My power has been trampled upon. The Shepherd has been crucified and Adam has been raised. I have been deprived of those whom I ruled. Those whom I swallowed in my strength I have given up. He who was crucified

has emptied the tombs. The power of death has been
vanquished." Glory to Your Cross and Resurrection,
O Lord. (Hymns of the Stichera of Great Saturday
Vespers)

The profound significance of this day is beautifully conveyed in a beloved fourth-century homily, the author of which remains unknown, but which may have been the inspiration for the traditional Orthodox icon of the Resurrection—the Descent into Hades:

Today there is a great silence over the earth, a great silence and stillness, a great silence because the King sleeps; the earth was fearful and was still, because God slept in the flesh and raised up those who were sleeping from ages before. God has died in the flesh, and the underworld trembles.

Truly He goes to seek out our first parent like a lost sheep; He wishes to visit those who sit in darkness and in the shadow of death. He goes to free the prisoner Adam and his fellow-prisoner

Eve from their pains, He who is God and Adam's son.

The Lord goes in to them holding His victorious weapon, His cross. When Adam, the first-created man, sees Him, he strikes his breast in terror and calls out to all, "My Lord be with you all." And Christ in reply says to Adam, "And with your spirit." And grasping his hand, He raises him up, saying, "Awake, O sleeper, and arise from the dead, and Christ shall give you light.

"I am your God, who for your sake became your son, who for you and your descendants now speak and command with authority those in captivity: Come forth! and those in darkness: Have light! and those who sleep: Arise!

"I command you: Awake, O sleeper; I did not make you to be held a prisoner in the underworld. Arise from the dead; I am the life of the dead. Arise, O man, work of My hands. Arise, you who were fashioned in My image. Rise, let us go hence; for you in Me and I in you, together we are one undivided person.

"For you, I Your God became your son; for

you, I the Master took on your form, that of a slave; for you, I who am above the heavens came on earth and under the earth; for you, O man, I became as a man without help, free among the dead; for you, who left a garden, I was handed over to the Jews from a garden and crucified in a garden.

"Look at the spittle on My face, which I received because of you, in order to restore you to that first divine inbreathing at creation. See the blows on My cheeks, which I accepted in order to refashion your distorted form to My own image. See the scourging of My back, which I accepted in order to disperse the load of your sins which was laid upon your back. See My hands nailed to the tree for a good purpose, for you, who stretched out your hand to the tree for an evil one.

"I slept on the cross and a sword pierced My side for you, who slept in paradise and brought forth Eve from your side. My side healed the pain of your side; My sleep will release you from your sleep in Hades; My sword has checked the sword which was turned against you.

"But arise, let us go hence. The enemy brought you out of the land of paradise; I will reinstate you, no longer in paradise, but on the throne of heaven. I denied you the tree of life, which was a figure, but now I Myself am united to you, I who am life. I posted the cherubim to guard you as they would slaves; now I make the cherubim revere you as they would gods.

"The cherubic throne has been prepared, the bearers are ready and waiting, the bridal chamber is in order, the food is provided, the everlasting houses and rooms are set; the treasures of good things have been opened; the kingdom of heaven has been prepared from before eternity."[19]

Just as the Vespers and the Liturgy of Great Saturday are two different services collapsed into one, so too the harrowing of hell and the Resurrection of our Lord are two themes that go hand in hand. The Vespers (the harrowing of hell) concludes

---

19 PG 43, 439, 462f

with the Old Testament readings and the Song of the Three Holy Youths:[20]

> *Praise the Lord and exalt Him above all unto the end of the ages.*

The Divine Liturgy follows, beginning with *As many as have been baptized into Christ have put on Christ. Alleluia!* in the place of the *Trisagion* that is normally chanted at the Liturgy before the New Testament readings. Then, after the epistle reading, we begin our first celebration of the Lord's Resurrection. This is why some Orthodox describe Great Saturday as "the first Resurrection." The priest proceeds around the church casting leaves and/or flowers among the congregation as we sing Psalm 81/82, with verse 8 as the jubilant refrain:

> *Arise, O God, judge the earth;*
> *For You shall inherit all nations.*

---

20 Daniel 3:57–88 (Septuagint)

The kingdom of death has been vanquished. "The firstborn from the dead" (Rev. 1:5) has gone forth from the tomb, and with Him He offers new and everlasting life to all who share in His humanity, to all the children of Adam.

⇴ 13 ⇴

The Great
and Holy Sabbath

GREAT AND HOLY SATURDAY

*Let all mortal flesh keep silence, and with fear and
trembling stand; let us take no thought for any
earthly thing; for the King of kings and Lord of lords
comes to be slain and given as food for the faithful.
(Cherubic Hymn of the Liturgy of Great and Holy
Saturday)*

So WE SING AT THE Divine Liturgy of St. Basil
the Great on Great and Holy Saturday. Through
prayer, we are to observe a "spiritual Sabbath,"
when we rest from all work to keep this day a

holy day dedicated to the Lord. Thus the Liturgy exhorts us to be inwardly silenced by this new Sabbath and to dedicate ourselves wholly to the things of the Spirit. Thus the Church prescribes for Great and Holy Saturday a strict fast (the only Saturday of the year on which we fast from oil) that we may not give too much time and thought even to food, but instead may give as much time and attention as possible to prayer and spiritual contemplation.

Our joy is almost complete. We have celebrated the destruction of Hades and the Resurrection of our Lord. But now the Church will invite us to place ourselves in the shoes of the myrrh-bearing women, who will go to the tomb of Christ to find it empty, and an angel declaring that Christ has risen. This is the theme of the Easter vigil on the night of Pascha. This is when we too begin to proclaim to the world the good news that "Christ has risen!"

↜ 14 ↝

Proclaim
the Good News

Great and Holy Pascha

We call the present Feast "Pascha," which in Hebrew means "Passing Over"; for this is the day on which God from the beginning brought the world out of nonexistence. On this same day He also made the people of Israel pass over the Red Sea and snatched them from the hands of Pharaoh. Again it was on this day that He came down from heaven and dwelt in the womb of the Virgin. And now He has snatched the whole of humanity from the vaults of Hell and lifted it up to heaven and brought it to its ancient dignity of incorruption. When He descended into Hell He raised all, but only as many as believed in

*Him were chosen. He freed the souls of the saints
since time began who were forcibly held fast by
Hell and made them all ascend to heaven. And so
we, rejoicing exceedingly, celebrate the Resurrection
with splendor as we mirror the joy with which our
nature has been enriched by God's compassionate
mercy. Likewise, to demonstrate the abolition of the
enmity and the union with God and the angels, we
give one another the customary kiss. (Synaxarion of
Great and Holy Pascha)*

On the eve of Easter Sunday, there is an
air of eager anticipation. The joy of Pascha is at
hand. We chant the canon of Great Saturday
with even greater joy, knowing that the end of
the Great Fast is upon us and the radiant feast of
Pascha has arrived. At the end of the canon, the
lights are extinguished, and in the midst of the
darkness we chant:

Behold, the darkness shall cover the earth,
And deep darkness the people;
But the LORD will arise over you,

And His glory will be seen upon you.
The Gentiles shall come to your light,
And kings to the brightness of your rising.
    (Is. 60:2–3)

Then the Paschal vigil begins, and the priest comes forth with a candle and sings:

Come, receive the light from the Unwaning Light,
and glorify Christ, who has risen from the dead.

This is repeated again and again as all come to receive the light, and as the flame of the Paschal vigil spreads throughout the church, so too does our joy and anticipation of the radiant celebration of our Lord's glorious Resurrection. This is more than a quaint religious custom: it is a reminder that we are the light of the world, and we are called to bear the good news of the Resurrection to all people. The light of this Paschal vigil represents the message of Christ risen from the dead, of which every one of us is a bearer. But if we are to be credible bearers of this good news, the light of Christ must be kindled within our hearts. As St. Gregory the Theologian writes:

> Yesterday I was crucified with Him; today I am glorified with Him; yesterday I died with Him; to-day I am quickened with Him; yesterday I was buried with Him; to-day I rise with Him. But let us offer to Him who suffered and rose again for us—you will think perhaps that I am going to say gold, or silver, or woven work or transparent and costly stones, the mere passing material of earth, that remains here below, and is for the most part always possessed by bad men, slaves of the world and of the Prince of the world. Let us offer ourselves, the possession most precious to God, and most fitting; let us give back to the Image what is made after the Image. Let us recognize our Dignity; let us honor our Archetype; let us know the power of the Mystery, and for what Christ died.
>
> Let us become like Christ, since Christ became like us. Let us become God's for His sake, since He for ours became Man. He assumed

the worse that He might give us the better; He became poor that we through His poverty might be rich; He took upon Him the form of a servant that we might receive back our liberty; He came down that we might be exalted; He was tempted that we might conquer; He was dishonored that He might glorify us; He died that He might save us; He ascended that He might draw to Himself us, who were lying low in the Fall of sin. Let us give all, offer all, to Him who gave Himself a Ransom and a Reconciliation for us. But one can give nothing like oneself, understanding the Mystery, and becoming for His sake all that He became for ours.[21]

Having received the light, a solemn procession with the Gospel is made, and we hear the Gospel reading of the feast:

Now when the Sabbath was past, Mary Magdalene, Mary *the mother* of James, and Salome

---

21 Gregory Nazianzen, *On Easter and His Reluctance*, Oration 1:4–5, Nicene and Post-Nicene Fathers, series II, vol. 7, Philip Schaff, Christian Classics Ethereal Library, p. 203.

bought spices, that they might come and anoint Him. Very early in the morning, on the first *day* of the week, they came to the tomb when the sun had risen. And they said among themselves, "Who will roll away the stone from the door of the tomb for us?"

But when they looked up, they saw that the stone had been rolled away—for it was very large. And entering the tomb, they saw a young man clothed in a long white robe sitting on the right side; and they were alarmed.

But he said to them, "Do not be alarmed. You seek Jesus of Nazareth, who was crucified. He is risen! He is not here. See the place where they laid Him. But go, tell His disciples—and Peter— that He is going before you into Galilee; there you will see Him, as He said to you." So they went out quickly and fled from the tomb, for they trembled and were amazed. And they said nothing to anyone, for they were afraid. (Mark 16:1–8)

Then we begin to sing again and again with inexhaustible joy:

> *Christ has risen from the dead. By death He has trampled upon death, and to those in the tombs He has given life.*

All is filled with light and gladness, as we proclaim the Lord's Resurrection, and we greet one another with the Paschal greeting, "Christ has risen!" "Truly the Lord has risen!" As the Church, the New Jerusalem, we are called to be filled with the light of Christ that we may truly be the light of the world:

> *Shine! Shine! O New Jerusalem! For the glory of the Lord has risen upon you! (Ninth ode of the Canon of Pascha)*

The joy is all the greater for those who have observed the fasts of Great Lent and Holy Week and who have participated in the Lenten worship: the long austere fast is over; the time for kneeling and prostrations has ended; religious disciplines have been relaxed.

But our joy cannot be complete without our full participation in the Eucharist, which concludes the Paschal vigil. It is therefore unfortunate that so many Orthodox Christians do not remain in the church for this Liturgy. Indeed, it is quite embarrassing that in some parishes, after the priest has sung the verse,

> Let God arise,
> Let His enemies be scattered;
> Let those also who hate Him flee before Him.
>   (Psalm 67/68:1)

half the congregation clears off!

Before Communion, we chant, *Receive the Body of Christ, and taste of the Immortal Spring* (Communion hymn for Pascha). The proof of the pudding is in the eating. To fully experience the joy of the Resurrection, we must receive Christ in the Eucharist. And while it is true that we cannot fully experience the joy of Pascha without first experiencing the ascetic struggle of Lent and

Holy Week, it remains the case that no matter how poorly we have observed them, we are all invited to rejoice in the Resurrection and to participate in the Easter Liturgy. This invitation is extended to us in the beautiful Paschal homily of St. John Chrysostom:

> Whoever is devout and loves God, let him enjoy this fair and shining festival. Whoever is a grateful servant, let him enter into the joy of his Lord. Have any wearied themselves with fasting? Let them now enjoy their payment. Has anyone labored since the first hour? Let him today receive his due. Did any come after the third hour? Let them feast with gratitude. Did any arrive after the sixth hour? Let them not hesitate, for there is no penalty. Did any delay until after the ninth hour? Let them approach without hesitating. Did any arrive only for the eleventh hour? Let them not fear because of their lateness, for the Lord is generous and receives the last as the first: He gives rest to the worker of the eleventh hour as to those of the first. He has

pity on the latter, He cares for the former. He gives to the one, He is generous to the other. He accepts the work done, He welcomes the intention. He honors the achievement, He praises the purpose.

Therefore all of you enter into the joy of our Lord: first and last, enjoy your reward. Rich and poor dance together. Sober and slothful honor the day. Fasters and non-fasters be glad today. The table is full; all of you enjoy yourselves. The calf is fatted; let none go away hungry. All of you enjoy the banquet of the faith. All of you enjoy the richness of His goodness. Let no one grieve at his poverty, for the kingdom for all has been revealed. Let no one bewail his faults, for forgiveness has risen from the tomb.

Let no one fear death, for the Savior's death has freed us. By enduring it, He quenched it. He who descended into Hell has despoiled Hell. He embittered it when it tasted His flesh, as Isaiah proclaimed in prophecy: "Death," he said, "was embittered when it met You there below." Embittered, for it was destroyed. Embittered, for it was mocked. Embittered, for it was slain.

Embittered, for it was wiped out. Embittered, for it was bound fast. It received a body and came face to face with God. It received earth and met heaven. It received what it saw and fell through what it did not see.

I said at the very beginning of this book that Holy Week brings the pious and the not-so-pious together. The invitation for all to come together to celebrate is most explicit in this sermon on Pascha night. Whether we have fasted and attended the services throughout Great Lent, or just from the beginning of Holy Week, or have only turned up for this midnight service, we are all invited to celebrate the feast with joy, without fear, hesitation, or guilt. No member of the Church is excluded. All our sorrows, all our failings, all our problems, all our sins disintegrate in the face of the Resurrection. By His Passion and Resurrection, Christ has freed us all. There can be no other response to this than joy and forgiveness:

This is the day of Resurrection; let us be radiant for the festival, and let us embrace one another. Let us say, brethren, even to those that hate us, "Let us forgive all things on the Resurrection." (Doxastikon of Great and Holy Pascha)

There is no greater liberation than forgiveness. When we truly understand the meaning of the Passion and Resurrection, when we really feel and live the joy of that freedom, forgiveness is the only possible response.

So if you are asking yourself, "What difference does all this make to the way I live my life?" let me help you answer that question: It makes every bit of difference! What cause now can we have to be angry with our neighbor? What cause to despair for our sins or fret about our problems? Who now has the right to look down on others? Who now has reason to complain that he is mistreated? Who now has cause to be bitter or bear a grudge? The universe has been filled with joy, freedom, and forgiveness:

> *Where, Death, is your sting? Where, Hell, is your victory? Christ has risen, and you are abolished! Christ has risen, and the demons have fallen! Christ has risen, and angels rejoice! Christ has risen, and life has found freedom! Christ has risen, and there is no corpse in the grave! For Christ, being raised from the dead, has become the first fruits of those who sleep. To Him be glory and might forever and ever. Amen. (Paschal homily of St. John Chrysostom)*

About the Author

ARCHIMANDRITE Vassilios Papavassiliou is a priest of the Greek Orthodox Archdiocese of Thyateira and Great Britain. He was born in London in 1977 and holds degrees in pastoral and social theology, classics, and Byzantine music. He is the author of *Meditations for Great Lent* (Conciliar Press/Ancient Faith Publishing, 2013), *Journey to the Kingdom: An Insider's Look at the Liturgy and Beliefs of the Eastern Orthodox Church* (Paraclete Press, 2012), *Meditations for Advent: Preparing for Christ's Birth* (Ancient Faith Publishing, 2013), *Thirty Steps to Heaven: The Ladder of Divine Ascent for All Walks of Life* (Ancient Faith Publishing, 2014) and numerous articles on Christian Orthodox faith and theology.

Ancient Faith Publishing hopes you have enjoyed and benefited from this book. The proceeds from the sales of our books only partially cover the costs of operating our nonprofit ministry—which includes both the work of **Ancient Faith Publishing** (formerly known as Conciliar Press) and the work of **Ancient Faith Radio.** Your financial support makes it possible to continue this ministry both in print and online. Donations are tax-deductible and can be made at www.ancientfaith.com.

To request a catalog of other publications,
please call us at (800) 967-7377 or (219) 728-2216
or log onto our website: **store.ancientfaith.com**

 ANCIENT FAITH RADIO

Bringing you Orthodox Christian music, readings,
prayers, teaching, and podcasts 24 hours a day since 2004
at **www.ancientfaith.com**

Other Books from Ancient Faith Publishing

Thirty Steps to Heaven
The Ladder of Divine Ascent for All Walks of Life
by Archimandrite Vassilios Papavassiliou

Many laypeople have attempted to read the great spiritual classic, *The Ladder of Divine Ascent,* but have been frustrated in attempting to apply the lessons of this monastic text in their everyday lives in the world. Archimandrite Vassilios interprets the *Ladder* for the ordinary Christian without sacrificing any of its beauty and power. Now you too can accept the challenge offered by St. John Climacus to ascend closer to God with each passing day.

Meditations for Great Lent
Reflections on the Triodion
by Archimandrite Vassilios Papavassiliou

The Lenten Triodion exhorts us, "Let us observe a fast acceptable and pleasing to the Lord." Using hymns from the Triodion and the Scripture readings appointed for the season, *Meditations for Great Lent* shows us how to make our fast acceptable: to fast not only from food but from sin; to fast with love and humility, as a means to an end and not an end in itself. Keep this gem of a book with you to inspire you for the Fast and to dip into for encouragement as you pursue your Lenten journey.

Meditations for Advent
Preparing for Christ's Birth
by Archimandrite Vassilios Papavassiliou

The author of *Meditations for Great Lent* takes us through the hymnography, Scripture readings, and iconography for the forty days leading up to the Nativity of Christ, showing how a full understanding of the Incarnation can enrich our spiritual lives.

Bread & Water, Wine & Oil
by Archimandrite Meletios Webber

According to two thousand years of experience, Orthodoxy shows us how to be transformed by the renewing of our mind—a process that is aided by participation in the traditional ascetic practices and Mysteries of the Church. In this unique and accessible book, Archimandrite Meletios Webber first explores the role of mystery in the Christian life, then walks the reader through the seven major Mysteries of the Orthodox Church, showing the way to a richer, fuller life in Christ.

The Scent of Holiness
by Constantina Palmer

Every monastery exudes the scent of holiness, but women's monasteries have their own special flavor. Join Constantina Palmer as she makes frequent pilgrimages to a women's monastery in Greece and absorbs the nuns' particular approach to their spiritual life. If you're a woman who's read of Mount Athos and longed to partake of its grace-filled atmosphere, this book is for you. Men will find it a fascinating read as well.

All titles available at store.ancientfaith.com. Most also available as ebooks.

The Ascetic Lives of Mothers

A Prayer Book for Orthodox Moms

by Annalisa Boyd

Ancient Faith Publishing

Contents

Introduction
  Making Time for Prayer ∾

The Asceticism of Mothers
  The "Rule" of Motherhood ∾
  The Virtues ∾

Daily Prayers
  Morning Prayers ∾
  Midday Prayers ∾
  Evening Prayers ∾

Prayers in Times of Trouble
  Addiction ∾
  Anger ∾
  Anxiety ∾
  Arguing ∾
  Complaining ∾
  Correction/Chastisement ∾
  Demonic Influence ∾
  Depression ∾
  Difficult Pregnancy ∾
  Disobedience ∾
  Enemies ∾
  Envy ∾
  Feeling of Failure (as a Parent) ∾
  Financial Strain ∾
  Greed/Selfishness ∾
  Homosexuality/Sexual Immorality ∾
  Idle Talking/Gossip ∾

Infertility ❧
Irritability ❧
Laziness ❧
Lying ❧
Persecution ❧
Pride ❧
Children with Special Needs ❧

Prayers for the Sick, Dying & Dead
He Restores My Soul—Prayers for the Sick ❧
The Valley of the Shadow—Prayers for the Dying ❧
The House of the Lord—Prayers for the Dead ❧

Confession and the Beatitudes
The Beatitudes ❧
Prayers before Confession ❧
Confession with Children ❧
Prayers after Confession ❧
A Word on Spiritual Fathers ❧

Prayers of Thanksgiving & Blessing
Before School ❧
Chastity ❧
Church ❧
Courage ❧
Diligence ❧
Faith ❧
Forgiveness ❧
Friendship ❧
Happiness ❧
Humility ❧
Liberality ❧
Love ❧

Patience/Longsuffering ∾

Peace ∾

Peaceful Sleep ∾

Safety ∾

Salvation ∾

Temperance ∾

Prayers Through the Stages of Motherhood

First-Time Mother ∾

Mother to Little Ones ∾

Mother to Older Children ∾

Mother to an Only Child ∾

Mother to a Large Family ∾

Mother to Adopted/Foster Children ∾

Prayer for Your Husband and Marriage ∾

Prayer of a Grandmother ∾

Prayers for Single Mothers ∾

Prayers for Godchildren & "Bonus" Children

Godchildren ∾

Stepchildren ∾

Prayers for the Future

Relationship with Christ and the Church ∾

Service in the Church ∾

Education ∾

Career ∾

As a Husband or Wife ∾

As a Father or Mother ∾

Calling to Ministry or Monasticism ∾

Introduction ∾

A~T THE TIME OF THE PRINTING OF THIS BOOK~, I will
have given birth to three, adopted five, fostered thirty, and
been godmother to five children. And still I'm no expert!
Whether you are mother to one child or fifteen, it is important to note that once you welcome a child into your life,
you will never be the same. From the time that child enters
your life—however that child enters your life—your whole
worldview shifts.

These precious gifts can be the cause of great joy, great
frustration, and great pain. But if we embrace it all "for the
joy set before us" (see Heb. 12:2), we will find even greater
comfort from the One who created our children. In our
Liturgy the priest says, "O Lord our God, Your power is
incomparable. Your glory is incomprehensible. Your mercy
is immeasurable. Your love for mankind is inexpressible." God's love for our children is wider and deeper and
stronger than even the wide, deep, strong love of a mother.

The prayers at the beginning of this book are those
prescribed by the Church. They have been written by the
Fathers of the Church and have been found to be acceptable

and beneficial in the official life of the Church. These, then, are the most important to pray and take to heart. Many of the other prayers throughout the book are simply prayers from the heart of one mama to another. While the other prayers in this book have been evaluated and approved by a priest, they are not the official prayers of the Church and should, therefore, be used for encouragement and to promote your own personal prayer time with our Lord.

I pray you will find comfort here to help you on your quest as you bring up your children in the way they should go, so that when they are grown they will not depart from it (Prov. 22:6).

Making Time for Prayer

You may have heard of Susanna Wesley, a godly mama from the late seventeenth to early eighteenth century. Susanna had nineteen children. Even in a time before television, internet, and soccer practice, this mama was busy! How on earth did she find time to pray?

The children were given a signal so they knew when mama was praying. When she sat down and put her apron up over her head, they knew not to interrupt her until that apron came down. The important thing wasn't the amount of time she spent praying, but the fact that she set aside even a brief moment to be present before the Lord.

While we won't necessarily throw an apron over our heads, giving our children proof that we have finally lost it, we can find moments in the midst of our busy lives to pray and be still.

When contemplating the "how" of prayer life, it can be hard to wade through the obstacles we face on a daily basis. On the one hand, we believe our loving God can make a way for us to meet with Him each day. On the other hand, we face so many interruptions along with real responsibilities. If we don't tend to them, who will? Should we give up trying if we happen to be a morning person or have developed adult-onset ADD (I'm only partially kidding)? Is it only possible to be successful if we follow a particular formula? As mothers, sometimes we have to get creative.

I used to be a night person, and for many years I'd fall asleep while in the process of trying to do my devotions at night. I'd get a few prayers in and find myself mixing prayers and nonsense words, to the amusement of my husband. Years into marriage and motherhood, I became a group leader for a women's Bible study. I had a lovely group of women I was committed to pray for, but I kept forgetting, or I'd start falling asleep before all their names were mentioned.

I had to do something drastic. This night-mama started getting up an hour before my children. Do you know what happened? Over the years I have become a morning person! I didn't believe it possible. The blessing and closeness with Christ this brought me were incredible. Each time I was successful in getting myself up early, I would find other moments throughout the day to pray or read a scripture verse to think on as I went about tending to the daily cares of my home.

Have I always been faithful in prayer? No. I have gone through spells where prayer felt almost like torture. It was dry and forced. But forced does not equate to unfruitful. Many times it is in the desert where we are most strengthened, and much good fruit is produced on the other end of those dry times—in spite of, or perhaps because of, the struggle.

Each mother is her own person with her own struggles and strengths. Your prayer time may look very different from mine. You may get up early in the morning to pray. You may stay up later (without falling asleep like me). You may be able to pray the hours each day. Or it may be all you can do to say one "Lord, have mercy on me, a sinner" with focus and sincerity. The point is to pray, to submit ourselves to Christ and trust He will make a way, if we are willing. Each of us needs to seek the counsel of our own spiritual mother or father, for God has placed these people in our lives to help us learn to run the race Christ has set before us with perseverance.

May the God of all creation, who blessed us with the children we have and knows the challenges we face each day, bless our time and provide a way for us to meet with Him each day. May He, as Metropolitan Philaret wrote, "pray Himself within me."